FIGHTING FORCES OF WORLD WAR II

IN THE AIR

John C. Miles

CAPSTONE PRESS
a capstone imprint

Edge Books are published by Capstone Press
1710 Roe Crest Drive, North Mankato, Minnesota 56003
www.mycapstone.com

Library of Congress Cataloging-in-Publication Data
Names: Miles, John C., author.
Title: Fighting Forces of World War II in the Air / by John C. Miles.
Other titles: Fighting Forces of World War Two in th Air
Description: North Mankato, Minnesota : Capstone Press, 2020. | Series: Edge Books. Fighting Forces of World War II | Includes bibliographical references and index. | Audience: Grades 4–6. | Audience: Ages 8–12.
Identifiers: LCCN 2018060643 | ISBN 9781543574821 (hardcover)
Subjects: LCSH: World War, 1939–1945—Aerial operations.
Classification: LCC D785 .M54 2020 | DDC 940.54/4—dc23
LC record available at https://lccn.loc.gov/2018060643

Summary: Explores the air forces that battled for control of the skies during World War II, and provides information about key battles, tactics, and weapons that helped propel the Allies to victory.

Editorial Credits
Editor: Julia Bird
Series designer: John Christopher/White Design
Photo researcher: Diana Morris

Photo Credits
Apic/Getty Images: 6-7c. Ivan Cholakov/Dreamstime: front cover t. Classic Stock/Alamy: front cover b, back cover, 1. cpaulfell/Shutterstock: 15t. Crown ©. MOD. Courtesy of Air Historical Branch (Royal Air Force): 20-21b. Gary Eason/Flight Artworks/Alamy: 25b. Everett Historical/Shutterstock: 4bl, 4tr, 5b, 13b, 14b, 29t. Flying Officer Jerry Fray, RAF. Wikimedia Commons: 21c. Getfree/Shutterstock: 12tl. Igor Golovniov/Shutterstock: 7br. Granger NYC/Alamy: 15b. Imperial Japanese Navy: 12b. IWM: 24tr. Interfoto/Alamy: 6bl. IWM/Getty Images: 16b. Keystone USA/Alamy: 26b, 27t. The Life Picture Collection/Getty Images: 8b. MAC1/Shutterstock: 21t. Leonard McCombe/Pictorial Press/IPC/Getty Images: 19tr. MPI/Getty Images: 28c. Richard Petersen/Alamy: 17b. Photoquest/Getty Images: 24b. Pictorial Press/Alamy: 10b, 25t. Popperfoto/Getty Images: 17t, 29b. Roger Viollet/Topfoto: 23b. Emir Simsek/Shutterstock: 26tl. Sovfoto/UIG/Getty Images: 5t, 23t. Reg Speller/Hulton Archive/Getty Images: 18b. SSPL/Getty Images: 19bl. UIG/Getty Images: 29c. Universal Art Archive/Alamy: 9t. U.S. Navy/Wikimedia Commons: 13c, 27c. WHA/Alamy: 9c, 12c, 27b. Nick Whittle/Shutterstock: 8c. Wiki-Ed/CC Wikimedia Commons: 11b. Wikimedia Commons: 6tl, 8tl, 10tl, 11t, 14tl, 16tl, 18tl, 20tl, 20c, 22tl, 22b, 24tl, 28t.

First published in Great Britain in 2018
by The Watts Publishing Group

Printed and bound in China
1593

Table of Contents

War Begins

In 1918 Germany lost World War I (1914–1918) and was forced to sign the Treaty of Versailles. Its harsh terms were very unpopular with Germans. In 1933 they elected a new leader, Adolf Hitler, who promised to restore Germany's standing in the world.

Hitler rides through cheering crowds in the German city of Kassel in 1939.

Rise of the Nazis

Hitler's Nazi (National Socialist) Party believed that their country should rule over all others and that certain groups of people, such as Jews, were trying to cheat Germany. Under the Nazis, Germany began to build up its armed forces and take over land in nearby countries. Finally, on September 1, 1939, German forces invaded neighboring Poland.

Allied Forces and Axis Powers

Great Britain, and the countries of its empire and dominions, joined France to declare war on Germany. These countries became known as the Allied forces. During 1940 Hitler took control of Denmark, Norway, France, Belgium, and the Netherlands. Italy joined the war on the side of the Nazis, forming the Axis powers. They were later bolstered by Japan. In June 1941 Germany invaded the Soviet Union. Then in December, Japan attacked a U.S. naval base, bringing the might of the United States into World War II (1939–1945).

Nazi dictator Adolf Hitler, pictured in the late 1930s.

Soviet Il-2 "Shturmovik" aircraft played a key role in the war by attacking German tanks.

The atomic "mushroom cloud" rises above Nagasaki, Japan.

The War Turns

Throughout 1942 and 1943, Allied and Axis forces battled in North Africa, Italy, the Soviet Union, and the Pacific as the war went global. Italy surrendered in September 1943. In June 1944 Allied forces launched Operation Overlord to begin taking back Europe. Months of fighting followed before the Allies began to advance toward Germany, something that the Soviet Union had begun to do from the east. Crushed in a massive pincer movement, Nazi forces were defeated. Hitler committed suicide at the end of April 1945 as Germany's capital, Berlin, fell to the Allies.

A TERRIBLE TOLL

The cost of the war in human lives was staggering. Historians estimate that more than 21–25 million soldiers and up to 55 million civilians were killed. Around 6 million were Jews who were murdered by the Nazis during the Holocaust.

The Atomic Bomb

In the Pacific the war had raged on. To end it, President Harry Truman authorized the use of the most terrible weapon ever invented—the atomic bomb—which obliterated the Japanese cities of Hiroshima and Nagasaki in August 1945. Japan finally surrendered. World War II was over.

World War II in the Air

Air forces fought in every battleground of World War II, from western Europe to North Africa and from the Pacific Islands to Burma. This book looks at just a few of the units that fought in the air during the war and gives details about some of their actions and the equipment they used.

THE LUFTWAFFE

FORMED:	STRENGTH:
1933	500,000 flying units (1941)
AREAS ACTIVE:	
Europe, Eastern Front, Mediterranean	

The Luftwaffe was the air force of Nazi Germany. Commanded by Hitler's deputy, Hermann Goering, the Luftwaffe played a leading role in Nazi victories throughout Europe in 1939 and 1940.

Air Power

After World War I it was apparent that aircraft would be a huge part of any future conflict. Rapid developments in aviation meant that by the 1930s flimsy biplanes with open cockpits were being replaced by metal monoplanes with closed cockpits. These aircraft could fly faster and higher and could carry more guns and bombs. They were much more deadly weapons.

During World War II many European towns and cities, such as this one in Poland, were reduced to rubble by air raids.

Luftwaffe Origins

At the end of World War I, the Treaty of Versailles banned Germany from having an air force. However, when Adolf Hitler came to power in 1933, he rejected the treaty and formed the Luftwaffe. He also set up the Air Ministry, in charge of developing new aircraft.

The Heinkel He-111 bomber aircraft was widely used by the Luftwaffe during World War II. It had a range of 1,430 miles (2,300 kilometers) and carried up to 4,400 pounds (2,000 kilograms) of bombs.

Planes and Tactics

During the mid-1930s, German factories began to produce some of the most advanced planes in the world, such as the Messerschmitt Bf 109 fighter. Then, in 1936, the Spanish Civil War (1936–1939) broke out. Hitler sent a large force to help Spanish right-wing fighters. Here, the Luftwaffe was able to try out its new weapons. By the late 1930s, it was one of the most experienced air forces in the world, with more than 4,200 planes.

Blitzkrieg!

In 1939 German forces swept into Poland. The Luftwaffe was a key part of the Nazi tactic known as *Blitzkrieg*, or "lightning war." Large bomber aircraft pounded targets such as airfields in front of advancing ground forces, while dive bombers and fighters destroyed tanks and smaller targets. Attacks were swift and terrifying. Countries such as Poland and France—both of which lacked modern air forces—fought bravely but didn't stand a chance.

Hermann Goering (left) and Luftwaffe general and ace pilot, Adolf Galland, tour an airfield during the war.

HERMANN GOERING

Hermann Goering (1893–1946) was a hero pilot of World War I. Joining the Nazis in the early 1920s, he rose to become Adolf Hitler's close associate. Goering oversaw Luftwaffe successes in Poland, France, the Netherlands, and the Balkans, as well as defeats in the Battle of Britain, North Africa, and the Soviet Union. He survived the downfall of Hitler and was put on trial for war crimes in 1946. Found guilty and sentenced to death, he committed suicide.

RAF FIGHTER COMMAND

	**FORMED:** 1936	**STRENGTH:** 1,208,000 (total, 1939–45) 185,000 (total airmen, 1939–45)
	AREAS ACTIVE: Europe	

After France fell to Nazi forces in 1940, Hitler planned to invade Great Britain next. Only the pilots of the Royal Air Force (RAF) Fighter Command stood in his way.

Re-Arming the RAF

Formed in 1936, Fighter Command was the branch of the RAF responsible for defending Great Britain's skies. The growing threat of Hitler led to Fighter Command being expanded. Its squadrons were equipped with two of the most famous and up-to-date planes of World War II—the Hawker Hurricane and the Supermarine Spitfire.

HURRICANES AND SPITFIRES

The Hawker Hurricane and the Supermarine Spitfire were developed in the 1930s. Both planes were powered by a single engine that delivered a top speed of more than 335 miles (540 km) per hour. Both were armed with wing-mounted, forward-firing machine guns. Both planes played a decisive role in the Battle of Britain as they battled with agile German Messerschmitt Bf 109s and other enemy aircraft.

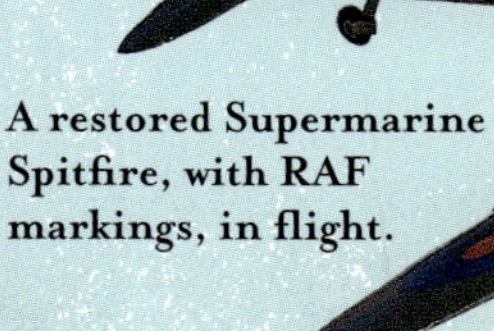

A restored Supermarine Spitfire, with RAF markings, in flight.

RAF pilots run or "scramble" to their Hurricanes during the Battle of Britain.

RADAR

Developed just before the war by scientist Robert Watson-Watt, radar (radio detection and ranging) was key to the RAF's success in the Battle of Britain. Radar stations located near the British coast detected enemy aircraft and provided commanders with details about the direction and speed of incoming enemy aircraft.

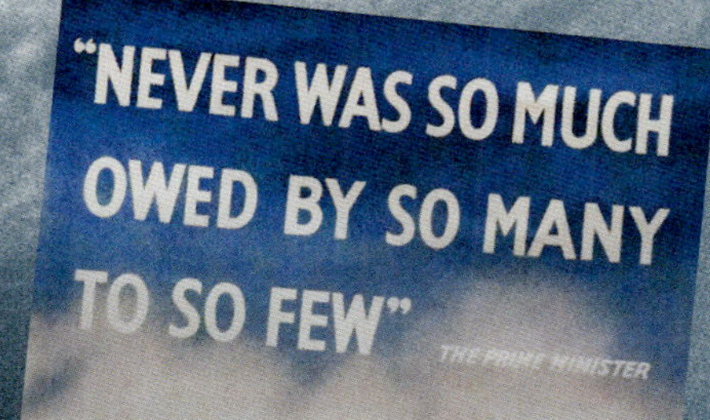

A squadron of Hawker Hurricanes takes to the skies during the Battle of Britain.

This wartime poster features British leader Winston Churchill's famous quote about the pilots of the RAF.

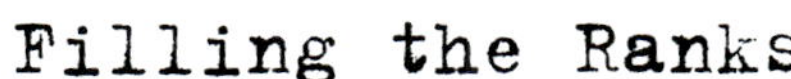

Filling the Ranks

Hundreds of young Allied pilots were quickly trained to take the place of those killed. In its battle with the Luftwaffe, the RAF was helped by pilots from New Zealand, Canada, Australia, and South Africa, as well as Poland, France, and the United States.

The Battle of Britain

Throughout the summer of 1940, the Battle of Britain raged in the skies over England as the planes of the RAF fought to the death with those of the Luftwaffe. Hitler had commanded Goering to destroy the RAF. Aerial battles took place almost daily between fighter planes, and both sides suffered heavy losses of men and equipment.

Change in Tactics

By October 1940 the RAF had narrowly won the Battle of Britain. Hitler postponed his planned invasion and instead ordered the Luftwaffe to bombard the British from the air by night. Between September 1940 and May 1941, cities and towns were hit again and again as the Nazis attempted to crush civilian morale. Thousands of people were killed or injured during the Blitz, as this campaign is known.

LUFTWAFFE FALLSCHIRMJÄGER

	**FORMED:** 1938	**STRENGTH:** 160,000
	AREAS ACTIVE: Europe, Eastern Front, Mediterranean	

During the war, both Allied and Axis forces used paratroopers to attack enemy positions from the air. The Fallschirmjäger, or "parachute-hunters," were the Luftwaffe's airborne infantry.

Early Successes

The first Fallschirmjäger division was formed in 1938 by Hermann Goering. The highly trained men first saw action early in the war during the German invasion of Poland, when they captured and held key airfields.

Belgian Bombardment

In April 1940 the Fallschirmjäger played a key role in the invasion and occupation of Denmark and Norway. Then on May 10, Fallschirmjäger deployed against the massive Belgian military fortress of Eben Emael. Here, the Luftwaffe landed nine gliders on the fort's roof before 85 Fallschirmjäger used flamethrowers, grenades, and demolition charges to completely overwhelm the fortress' 800 defenders in just a few hours.

Adolf Hitler surrounded by the Fallschirmjäger who successfully captured Eben Emael.

Junkers Ju52s of the Luftwaffe flying in formation.

The Battle of The Hague

While the assault on Eben Emael was taking place, in the Netherlands, German commanders sent Fallschirmjäger units to capture airfields before attempting an assault on the Dutch capital, The Hague. However, fierce resistance inflicted heavy casualties on the Fallschirmjäger, killing up to 400 men. The units failed to take The Hague as planned, and more than 120 transport aircraft were destroyed.

Crete

The next big operation for Fallschirmjäger units was to attack the strategically important Mediterranean island of Crete in May 1941. More than 20,000 Fallschirmjäger landed on the island, but in only nine days of fighting, more than 3,250 were killed and 3,400 wounded. Although Crete eventually fell to the Nazis, it is said that Hitler, horrified at the scale of these losses, refused to approve any further large-scale airborne operations.

Elite Fallschirmjäger units continued to fight bravely as ground troops during the rest of World War II, supporting Nazi forces wherever they were engaged.

JUNKERS Ju52

- **LOAD** 18 Fallschirmjäger
- **RANGE** 620 miles (1,000 km)

The Luftwaffe's main transport plane was the tough and reliable Junkers Ju52. Powered by three BMW engines, the aircraft could carry 18 fully equipped Fallschirmjäger. It could also tow two gliders, which were often used to deliver paratroopers to their targets. When formed in 1938, the 7th Air Division had 250 Ju52s. During World War II more than 2,800 were built.

Fallschirmjäger attack Crete on May 20, 1941, as a Ju52, hit by antiaircraft fire, plunges to the ground.

THE IMPERIAL JAPANESE NAVY 1ST AIR FLEET

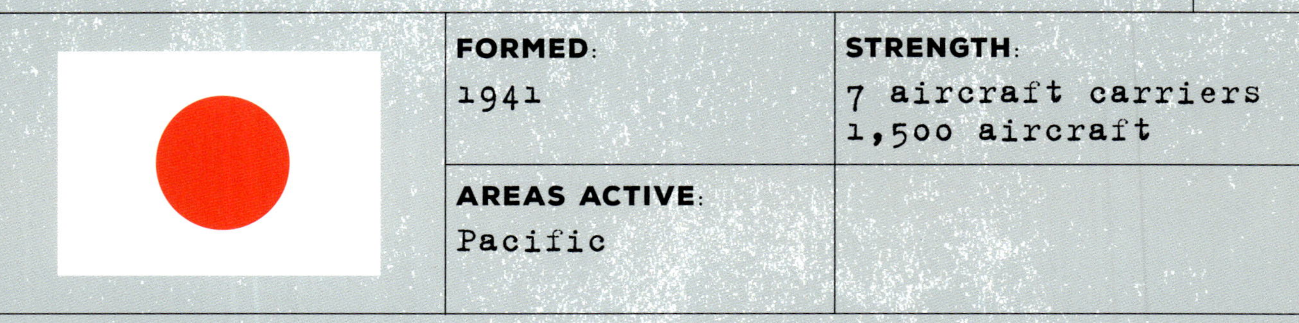

	FORMED:	STRENGTH:
	1941	7 aircraft carriers 1,500 aircraft
	AREAS ACTIVE:	
	Pacific	

In 1941 the Imperial Japanese Navy created the 1st Air Fleet. At that time, it was the world's most powerful naval aviation force.

Pearl Harbor

The 1st Air Fleet burst into the war when it attacked the U.S. naval base at Pearl Harbor, Hawaii, on December 7, 1941. Japan's main motive was to stop the United States from interfering with Japan's ambitions to take over southeast Asia. The operation's strike force included six aircraft carriers, two battleships, three cruisers, and nine destroyers. The carriers launched fighters, dive bombers, and torpedo bombers, which fired torpedoes at enemy ships.

Japanese Vice-Admiral Chuichi Nagumo commanded the attack.

The aircraft carrier *Kaga* was part of Japan's Pearl Harbor task force.

AIRCRAFT CARRIERS

These floating airbases were especially useful to military powers during World War II because aircraft couldn't travel very far before they ran out of fuel. Carriers extended the strike range of an air force by putting its planes closer to vital targets. Because they were very large and had relatively few guns, carriers were vulnerable to enemy attack.

A Devastating Attack

The force set sail on November 26, 1941. Just before 8:00 a.m. on Sunday, December 7, Nagumo struck, sending in the first of two waves of Japanese planes against the ships of the U.S. Pacific fleet and its naval base. By the end of the day, 21 U.S. ships had been sunk or crippled, 188 planes on the base's airfield had been destroyed, and more than 3,500 U.S. personnel had been killed or wounded. The United States declared war on Japan the next day.

More Operations

Later in the war, the 1st Air Fleet took part in many key battles in the Pacific against Allied forces, including the Battle of Midway in 1942. This latter action resulted in the loss of four Japanese carriers, along with most of their airmen. By the time of the Battle of Leyte Gulf in October 1944, the Japanese carrier fleet had suffered further losses and had few pilots or planes left. Its remaining carriers, including one survivor of the attack on Pearl Harbor, were sunk by U.S. air attacks.

NAKAJIMA B5N2 "KATE" TORPEDO BOMBER

- **RANGE** 1,238 miles (1,992 km)
- **TOP SPEED** 235 miles (378 km) per hour
- **CREW** 3

The Nakajima B5N2 "Kate" was the Imperial Japanese Navy's standard carrier-based torpedo bomber of World War II. The B5N2 was armed with one 1,760-pound (800-kg) torpedo or an armor-piercing bomb, plus machine guns. Nearly 150 "Kates" took part in the Pearl Harbor attack.

More than 1,100 "Kates" were built.

The battleship USS *Arizona* ablaze and sinking after the Japanese attack on Pearl Harbor.

DOOLITTLE'S RAIDERS

	**FORMED:** 1942	**STRENGTH:** 16 bombers 80 airmen
	AREAS ACTIVE: Pacific	

Five months after the attack on Pearl Harbor, a daring raid by U.S. aircraft struck at the heart of Japan, bombing its capital, Tokyo, and four other cities.

Roosevelt's Revenge

President Franklin Roosevelt wanted to bomb Japan in order to boost U.S. morale, which was at an all-time low after the Pearl Harbor attack. Roosevelt also wished to let the Japanese people know that they were not invincible.

Doolittle Takes Charge

The officer tasked with organizing and leading the raid was experienced airman Colonel James Doolittle. He planned to launch 16 B-25B Mitchell medium bombers from the carrier USS *Hornet*. Each plane would be modified to carry extra fuel, plus four 496-pound (225-kg) bombs. The *Hornet* set sail from San Francisco on April 2, 1942. By April 18 the carrier was nearing the attack position 620 miles (1,000 km) from Japan.

One of Doolittle's B-25s, bound for Tokyo, takes off from the flight deck of the USS *Hornet*.

A restored B-25 in flight

B-25 MITCHELL MEDIUM BOMBER

- **LOAD** 1,980 pounds (900 kg)
- **RANGE** 2,730 miles (4,400 km) (B-25B; specially modified version)

The B-25 Mitchell medium bomber served Allied forces in every area during World War II. It was a very successful design and more than 9,800 aircraft were built. The specially modified version used in the Doolittle raid had a five-man crew and carried 6,830 pounds (3,100 kg) of fuel and 1,980 pounds (900 kg) of bombs.

Attack!

As Doolittle's B-25s approached the Japanese coast, they dropped to wave height to avoid being spotted. Then they swept in over Tokyo and, despite antiaircraft fire and attacks by Japanese fighter planes, managed to hit most of their targets. They even shot down some Japanese planes. None of the U.S. bombers were destroyed.

What Happened Next

After the raid, the planes headed southwest, where they were supposed to land at prearranged bases in China. But bad weather and low fuel meant that this plan had to be abandoned. One bomber flew to the nearby Soviet Union, where its crew was captured. The remaining 15 planes reached China, where they crash-landed. Most of the men, including Doolittle, were rescued. However, some died in the crash landings and the rest were captured by Japanese forces. Although Doolittle saw the raid as a failure, it boosted U.S. morale as Roosevelt had planned and put the mighty Japanese war machine on the defensive. Doolittle was awarded the U.S. Medal of Honor and was promoted to Lieutenant-General.

President Franklin Roosevelt awards Colonel James Doolittle the U.S. Medal of Honor in May 1942.

RAF BOMBER COMMAND

FORMED:
1936

STRENGTH (1939):
23 squadrons
280 aircraft

AREAS ACTIVE:
Europe

Working alongside the U.S. Army Air Forces, RAF Bomber Command attacked critical targets in Germany until the very end of the war.

RAF armorers wheel a cart of 990-pound (450-kg) bombs to a waiting Handley Page Halifax bomber.

Bombing Expands

Formed in 1936, Bomber Command was a key part of the Royal Air Force, but early battles exposed its dated equipment. Starting in 1942, Great Britain began attacking German industries and cities from the air. Bomber Command's planes were modernized, and better aircraft, such as the Handley Page Halifax and Avro Lancaster, replaced older models. These newer planes had four engines, carried massive bomb loads, and had a much greater range. Improvements in radar and navigation systems helped airmen locate their targets more accurately.

Another innovation was the introduction of Pathfinders. These specialist squadrons flew ahead of the main force and dropped flares to guide the bombers to their targets.

AIRMEN

Each RAF heavy bomber was crewed by up to seven men. Airmen came from Great Britain and many other countries. For example, Number 6 Group was an all-Canadian unit. Personnel from New Zealand, Australia, Poland, and many other nations also served. Flying bombing missions was highly dangerous. Out of every 100 men serving with Bomber Command, 55 were killed or died of their wounds.

The Canadian crew of an RAF Halifax bomber poses in front of their aircraft.

The ruins of Dresden after the February 1945 raid.

Raids Increase

As the war continued, attacks on Germany increased. The Ruhr industrial region was hit in March 1943. In July more than 800 RAF and U.S. bombers attacked the city of Hamburg, killing more than 42,000. The following winter Bomber Command hit the German capital, Berlin, and in 1944 attacked targets in support of the D-Day landings. In late 1944 RAF and U.S. forces heavily bombed the cities of Duisburg and Brunswick. And in 1945 Bomber Command carried out operations, such as the massive raid on Dresden. Its attacks disrupted the production of Nazi war supplies and diverted planes and guns away from war fronts back home to defend Germany.

AIR TRANSPORT AUXILIARY

	**FORMED:** 1940	**STRENGTH:** 1,318 pilots 2,786 ground staff
	AREAS ACTIVE: Great Britain, Europe	

During World War II, the pilots of Great Britain's Air Transport Auxiliary (ATA) moved aircraft to where they were needed, freeing up RAF pilots for front-line combat.

Origins

The Air Transport Auxiliary was formed in 1940, using civilian pilots. At first it was planned that ATA staff would transport only mail and medical supplies, but it soon became necessary for them to take on other duties. These included moving planes between factories, delivering new aircraft to combat units, both in Great Britain and overseas, and flying damaged aircraft back to manufacturers for repairs.

Who Flew?

The ATA included pilots who were unfit for combat duties with the RAF, but could still fly. Some of the pilots had physical disabilities, weak eyesight, or had surpassed the age limit to fight. ATA pilots jokingly referred to the organization as "Ancient and Tattered Airmen."

Workers build de Havilland Mosquito aircraft at a factory. The ATA delivered completed planes to RAF squadrons.

Training

ATA pilots initially trained at the RAF's Central Flying School, but the ATA soon developed its own training programs. Once pilots were qualified to fly one type of aircraft, they gained experience by flying every model of that aircraft before moving on to another type. By the end of World War II, ATA pilots had flown almost every plane in service with the RAF, including the biggest bombers.

Women pilots were featured in wartime magazines, helping to popularize the ATA's vital work.

Women Pilots

A large proportion of ATA pilots were women—the first female ATA pilots took to the air on January 1, 1940. The women of the ATA came from many different nations including Canada, South Africa, the United States, Australia, New Zealand, the Netherlands, and Poland. By the end of the war, 166 women had flown with the ATA.

AMY JOHNSON

Born in 1903, Amy Johnson (left) was a pioneering woman aviator who gained her pilot's license in 1929. In the 1930s she became a celebrity due to her record-breaking flights which crisscrossed the world, including the first female solo flight to Australia. Johnson joined the ATA in 1940, but in January 1941 her plane flew off-course in bad weather, ran out of fuel, and crashed into the Thames River. Johnson's body was never found. Mystery surrounds the purpose of her final flight, which is still a government secret.

RAF 617 SQUADRON "DAMBUSTERS"

	FORMED: 1943	**STRENGTH:** 16 bombers 133 airmen
	AREAS ACTIVE: Europe	

In 1943 Allied commanders planned a daring raid that stretched both the RAF and the technology of the time to their limits.

The Targets

Before the war the British Air Ministry had identified the industrial area of the Ruhr Valley, in northwestern Germany, as a key target. The steelworks and factories located there needed large amounts of electricity and water, which were supplied in part by three huge dams—the Möhne, Eder, and Sorpe. Allied leaders determined that if holes could be blasted in the dams, the resulting floods would hit the Nazi war machine hard.

Barnes Wallis served as a Sub-Lieutenant in the Royal Naval Air Service during World War I.

Bouncing Bomb

To breach the dams the RAF turned to brilliant engineer Barnes Wallis. Wallis faced two major problems—no aircraft was capable of carrying bombs big enough to do the job, and the dams were protected by huge nets. Wallis believed that smaller bombs might work if they could be skipped across the water like stones to avoid the nets, before sinking and exploding underwater against the dam. Tests proved him correct.

The airmen of 617 Squadron pose in front of an Avro Lancaster in 1943.

Ambitious Mission

To conduct the raid, the RAF formed a new unit, 617 Squadron, equipped with Avro Lancasters. Each crew had to fly at a height of only 61 feet (18.5 meters) and a speed of exactly 217 miles (350 km) per hour before releasing one bomb 394 yards (360 m) from the target.

The planes were specially modified for the mission. To achieve the bouncing action, a motor had to spin the 8,800-pound (4,000-kg) bomb before its release.

AVRO LANCASTER

- **LOAD** 14,330 pounds (6,500 kg)
- **RANGE** 1,550 miles (2,500 km)

One of the most successful aircraft of the war, the Avro Lancaster heavy bomber first entered service with the RAF in 1942. The plane had a crew of seven and a range of more than 1,550 miles (2,500 km). It carried around 14,330 pounds (6,500 kg) of bombs on an average mission.

The Dambusters

On May 16, 1943, 19 bomber crews of the 617 Squadron set off on their mission. Some planes were hit by antiaircraft fire and crashed before they reached Germany. However, several of the aircraft managed to release their bombs successfully. The Möhne Dam and the Eder Dam were both breached, and water flooded the valleys below, knocking out power stations, disrupting Nazi industrial production for months, and killing more than 1,000 civilians. The Sorpe Dam was damaged but not breached. The raid had been a success, but it had a high cost—out of the 133 airmen who set off on the mission, 53 were killed and three taken prisoner.

The breached Möhne Dam, with water pouring through it.

SHTURMOVIK GROUND-ATTACK SQUADRONS

	**FORMED:** 1939	**STRENGTH:** 36,000 planes
	AREAS ACTIVE: Eastern Front	

In June 1941 Nazi troops swept into the Soviet Union in the biggest land invasion in history. The Soviet Il-2 "Shturmovik" ground-attack squadrons played a key role in the conflict.

Into Combat

Shturmovik pilots first went into battle shortly after the Nazi invasion in 1941. Their initial missions were disastrous—the attacking units lost 55 out of their 65 aircraft. However, after a review of tactics, Il-2 pilots became skilled at destroying German tanks. Then the armored Shturmovik aircraft came into its own. The planes would fly in low, often making several slow passes under heavy fire before launching rockets or dropping bombs. The pilots needed nerves of steel and top-notch flying skills.

Shturmovik Pilots

Ivan Grigorevich Drachenko was one of the most successful Il-2 pilots of the war. He took part in the Battle of Kursk in 1943 but was wounded and taken prisoner by German forces. Drachenko escaped to fly again, completing more than 150 missions and destroying 76 German tanks. Drachenko was one of only four men to be awarded the Soviet Order of Glory three times and was proclaimed a Hero of the Soviet Union. A famous female pilot was Anna Yegorova (right), also a Hero of the Soviet Union. She flew 277 missions before she was shot down and badly wounded. Believed dead, Yegorova was discovered alive in a prison camp at the end of the war.

Il-2 Shturmoviks in flight. Although pilots were well protected by steel armor, the aircraft's rear gunners were dangerously exposed to enemy fire.

IL-2 SHTURMOVIK

- **RANGE** 445 miles (720 km)
- **LOAD** 4 X 218-pound (99-kg) bombs

The Il-2 Shturmovik was the brainchild of Soviet aircraft designer Sergey Ilyushin. Much of the Il-2 was reinforced with protective steel armor, earning it the nickname "The Flying Tank." The Il-2 had a crew of two and was armed with either eight 82-mm rockets or four 218-pound (99-kg) bombs. The plane also had one forward-facing cannon on each wing and one machine gun pointing backward to defend the tail from enemy fighter attack.

Shturmovik planes launch an attack on German tanks.

Kursk

This epic battle, in which the Il-2 played a large part, took place during July and August 1943, when German tank forces attacked well-defended Soviet positions at Kursk, 280 miles (450 km) southwest of Moscow. The missions flown by Shturmovik pilots made a big contribution to halting the German advance. They flew in formations of up to eight planes, from which a single aircraft would swoop down in turn to attack German tanks and then return to the formation.

ALLIED AIRBORNE DIVISIONS, D-DAY

	FORMED:	**STRENGTH:**
 	1942 (101st Airborne) 1943 (6th Airborne)	6,000 (101st) 16,000 (6th)
	AREAS ACTIVE: Europe	

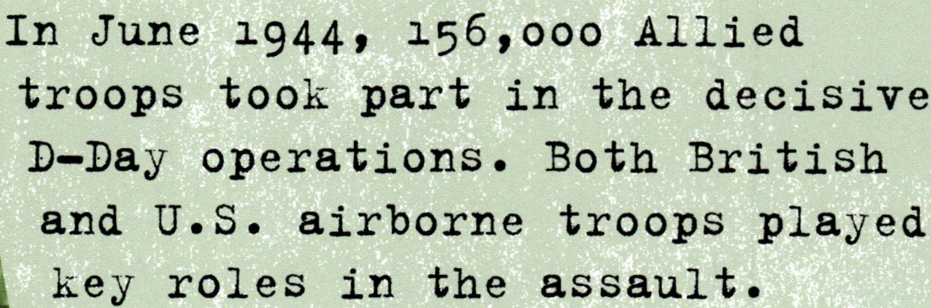

In June 1944, 156,000 Allied troops took part in the decisive D-Day operations. Both British and U.S. airborne troops played key roles in the assault.

D-Day

Allied forces trained for months for the attack on Nazi-occupied France known as Operation Overlord or D-Day. In the early hours of June 6, a huge task force crossed the English Channel to take part in the biggest seaborne invasion in history. Five Normandy beaches—code-named Utah, Omaha, Gold, Juno, and Sword—were chosen for the landings. German resistance was fierce, and thousands of soldiers were killed or wounded as they waded ashore. Despite the casualties, by the end of the day the Allies had secured the beaches.

Early Success

Elite airborne units landing by parachute and glider were the first soldiers in action on D-Day. Units from Great Britain's 6th Airborne landed near Sword Beach at 12:15 a.m., tasked with capturing two vital bridges, destroying a battery of heavy guns, and blowing up five other bridges that would have allowed the Germans to counter-attack. The force assigned to the Caen Canal bridge seized it in just 10 minutes. Other units soon took the Orne River bridge.

U.S. paratroopers crowd into a C-47 transport aircraft on their way into action on D-Day.

Two members of the 6th Airborne hold a crossroads on D-Day. Their Horsa glider sits in the background.

Challenges

Things didn't go so well for the parachute battalion assigned to capture the gun battery. An aerial bombardment by the RAF had failed, and some of the unit's vital equipment gliders had crashed into the sea. Nevertheless, the battery was taken. The troops ordered to destroy the bridges also experienced problems—the bad weather caused the men to be scattered over a wide area—but eventually the five bridges were destroyed.

101st Airborne

The bad weather also affected the U.S. 101st Airborne Division at Utah Beach, where troops were tasked with seizing four narrow routes that led off the beach. Many of the division's airborne troops were scattered by the weather and landed in the wrong places. Despite this, hastily assembled groups of 101st Airborne troops captured German positions and held them until support arrived.

DOUGLAS C-47 DAKOTA

One of the most successful aircraft ever, the rugged C-47 was used throughout the war as a paratroop and cargo aircraft and was vital to the success of many Allied campaigns. It carried 28 airborne troops or 18 stretchers, and it had a range of 1,550 miles (2,500 km).

Painted with striped markings to avoid friendly fire, RAF C-47 aircraft drop paratroopers on D-Day.

KAMIKAZE SQUADRONS

FORMED:	STRENGTH:
1944	11,600
AREAS ACTIVE: Pacific	

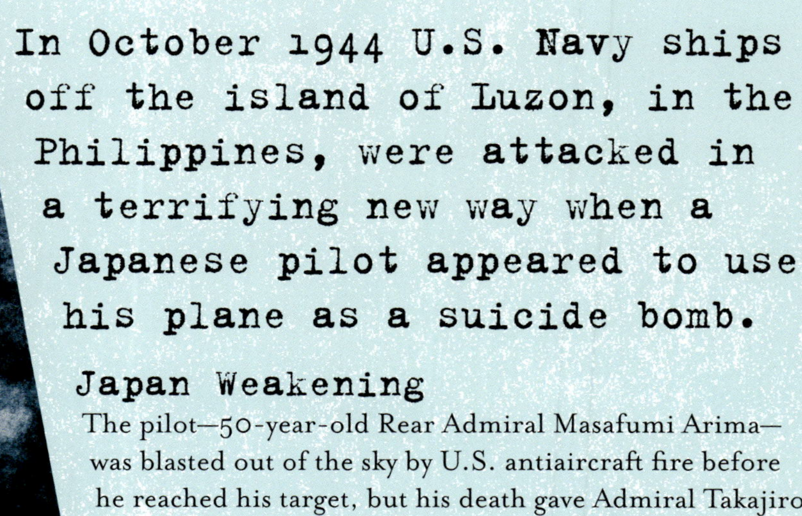

In October 1944 U.S. Navy ships off the island of Luzon, in the Philippines, were attacked in a terrifying new way when a Japanese pilot appeared to use his plane as a suicide bomb.

Japan Weakening

The pilot—50-year-old Rear Admiral Masafumi Arima—was blasted out of the sky by U.S. antiaircraft fire before he reached his target, but his death gave Admiral Takajiro Onishi, the new commander of the Imperial Japanese Navy's First Air Fleet, an idea. Japan had suffered huge losses of both pilots and aircraft, and weakened Japanese industries could no longer produce large numbers of up-to-date planes. With the Allies closing in, the Admiral believed that young pilots should be given the chance to volunteer to die for Japan by flying their bomb-laden aircraft straight into Allied warships.

Kamikaze

In Japanese military culture there had always been a tradition of preferring death to surrender. The new suicide squadrons became known as *Kamikaze*, or "divine wind." This referred to a failed invasion of Japan by the Mongols in 1281, when a huge windstorm wrecked the enemy's fleet. Legend attributed the wind to the gods.

Shot down before reaching his target—a U.S. aircraft carrier—a Kamikaze pilot crashes into the Pacific.

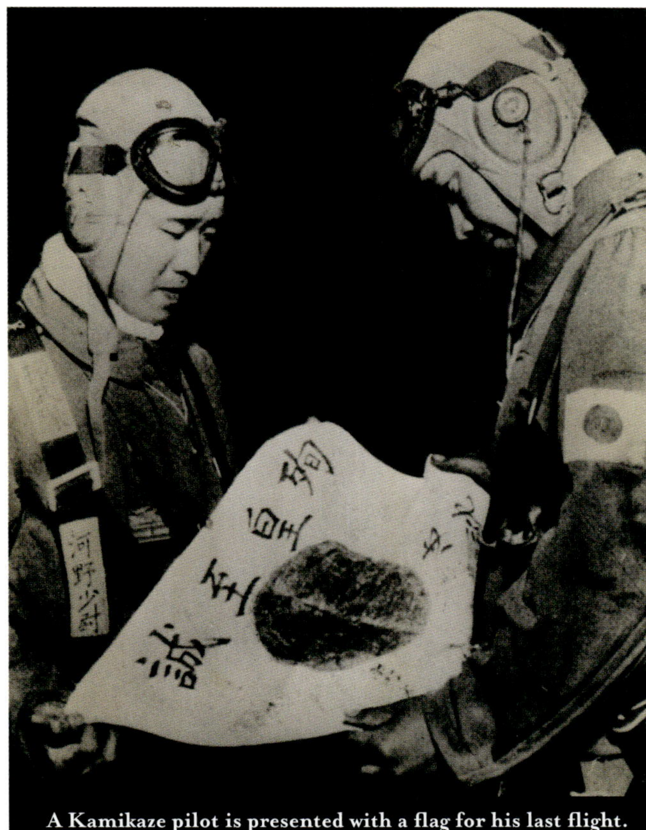

A Kamikaze pilot is presented with a flag for his last flight.

Final Phase

Japanese suicide attacks reached their peak in the Battle of Okinawa in April to June 1945, when more than 30 U.S. warships were sunk or heavily damaged. The British Pacific Fleet was hit as well, when aircraft carrier HMS *Formidable* was attacked on May 4, 1945. In this case, the ship's armored flight deck proved its worth—damage was small and casualties few. Although terrifying at the time, most of the Allied ships lost were smaller vessels such as destroyers, so the tragic bravery of Japan's Kamikaze pilots in fact made little difference to the outcome of the war.

Desperate Measure

Many young pilots volunteered for the suicide squadrons. They were treated like heroes, toasted with *sake*, or rice wine, and photographed wearing a ceremonial *hakimachi*, or headscarf, before their fatal mission. Attacks on Allied ships soon became more frequent. In the Battle of Leyte Gulf on October 25, the U.S. aircraft carrier *St. Lo* sank when it was hit and the resulting fire exploded its bomb magazine. By the end of the day on October 26, five U.S. ships had been sunk and 23 heavily damaged by more than 55 Kamikaze attacks.

YOKOSUKA MXY7 OKHA

Japan built more than 850 of these piloted bombs. Packed with explosives, the Okha, or "cherry blossom," was slung beneath a bomber, which transported the weapon to the target area. When released, the suicide pilot dropped into a glide before igniting the bomb's three rocket motors to power it at more than 373 miles (600 km) per hour into its target.

Kamikaze pilot Lieutenant Yamaguchi crashes his aircraft into the carrier USS *Essex* on November 25, 1944, killing 15 and wounding 44.

509TH COMPOSITE GROUP

	FORMED: 1944	STRENGTH: 1,767
	AREAS ACTIVE: Pacific	

By mid-1945 Japan faced an Allied invasion but refused to surrender. In late July, President Harry Truman authorized the use of the atomic bomb against Japan.

A "Little Boy" type of atomic bomb

The Manhattan Project

Starting in 1942, scientist J. Robert Oppenheimer led the team at Los Alamos Laboratory in New Mexico that developed the atomic bomb—a weapon of unimaginable destructive power, fueled by enriched uranium. On July 16, 1945, a test explosion proved that the deadly weapon worked. Two types of atomic bomb—code-named "Little Boy" and "Fat Man"—were prepared for use.

Closing In

In 1945 the United States unleashed a massive bombing campaign against Japan, hitting cities hard. The bombing of Tokyo in March 1945 alone killed around 100,000 people. The subsequent capture of the Japanese island of Okinawa made an Allied invasion more likely. But the war in the Pacific had proved that the Japanese preferred death to surrender. An invasion was going to be a long campaign, costing hundreds of thousands more lives.

Preparing the Bombs

The 509th Composite Group was the group tasked with delivering the bombs. Equipped with specially upgraded B-29 bombers, the unit was commanded by Colonel Paul Tibbets. By May 1945 the force was in place on the Pacific island of Tinian.

The "Fat Man" atomic bomb dropped on Nagasaki by the B-29 *Bockscar* on August 9, 1945, created an 11-mile- (18-km-) high mushroom cloud.

Hiroshima

The order authorizing the use of nuclear weapons was issued on July 25, 1945. Hiroshima, a key industrial center, was chosen as the first target. On August 6 Tibbets piloted his B-29, *Enola Gay*, to the city and dropped the first atomic bomb. The massive blast produced a blinding flash and, over the next few hours, a massive firestorm. More than 90,000 people were killed. Many more thousands died of burns and radiation sickness.

Colonel Paul Tibbets stands in front of his plane *Enola Gay*—which was named after his mother.

Nagasaki

Despite the destruction, the Japanese didn't surrender so the 509th dropped another atomic bomb on the port city of Nagasaki on August 9. Up to 80,000 people were killed and many thousands more died later. Japan announced its surrender on August 15. Its delegates signed the official document on September 2. World War II was finally over.

ATOMIC DEBATE

To this day the use of the atomic bombs in 1945 remains highly controversial. Some argue that it was the only way to end the war quickly. Others say Japan would have surrendered eventually and that the use of such terrible weapons was a crime against humanity.

Glossary

aircraft carrier (AIR-kraft KA-ree-ur)—a large warship used as a floating airbase

Allied forces (AL-lyd FORSS-uhs)—the military forces of Great Britain, its empire and dominions, France and, after 1941, the Soviet Union and the United States

Axis powers (AK-siss POU-urz)—the military forces of Nazi Germany, Italy, Japan, and some other countries

battery (BA-tuh-ree)—a group of large guns in the same place

biplane (BYE-plane)—an aircraft with two wings, one above the other

Blitzkrieg (BLITS-kreeg)—a Nazi invasion strategy where air and ground forces worked together to quickly overwhelm a country's defenders

breach (BREECH)—to make a big hole in something

civilian (si-VIL-yuhn)—a person who is not in the armed forces

cockpit (KOK-pit)—the part of an aircraft from which the plane is controlled by its crew

cruiser (KROOZ-ur)—a medium-sized warship armed with heavy guns

demolition (de-muh-LI-shuhn)—blowing up military targets with explosives

deploy (di-PLOY)—to send into action

destroyer (di-STROI-ur)—a small, fast warship armed with light guns

dictator (DIK-tay-tuhr)—a leader who wields supreme power to control a country and its people

dive bomber (DIVE BOM-ur)—an aircraft that releases its bombs in a steep dive

dominions (duh-MIN-yuhnz)—countries that in the past were part of the British Empire, but had their own government

empire (EM-pire)—a group of countries under the control of a single government or ruler

firestorm (FYR-storm)—when repeated bombing creates a tornado of fire that sucks up everything in its path

flamethrower (FLAYM-throh-uhr)—a weapon that shoots out blazing fuel

glider (GLYE-dur)—a lightweight aircraft without an engine that is towed to its destination by a powered plane

grenade (gruh-NAYD)—a small bomb thrown by hand

heavy bomber (HEV-ee BOM-ur)—a four-engined aircraft that carried a massive bomb load

Holocaust (HOL-uh-kost)—the mass murder of millions of Jews, as well as gypsies, the disabled, homosexuals, and political and religious leaders during World War II

invincible (in-VIN-suh-buhl)—able to do anything or behave in any way without punishment

Timeline

1939

September 1 Nazi Germany invades Poland; World War II begins

September 3 Great Britain and France declare war on Germany

September British Expeditionary Force (BEF) sails for France

1940

April/May Nazi Germany invades Denmark and Norway

May 10 Nazi Germany invades the Netherlands, Belgium, and France

May 26 the Allied evacuation at Dunkirk, Operation Dynamo, begins

June 11 Italy joins the war on the Axis side

June 22 France signs an armistice with Nazi Germany

July 10–October 31 The Battle of Britain—Great Britain's Royal Air Force defeats Nazi Luftwaffe

September 1940–May 1941 Nazi "Blitz" (aerial bombing campaign) on Great Britain

December Great Britain defeats Italian forces in North Africa

1941

February Hitler sends Rommel's Afrika Korps to North Africa

April Italy and Germany attack Yugoslavia, Greece, and Crete

June 22 Nazis invade Soviet Union

December 7 Japanese attack Pearl Harbor; United States enters war on Allied side

December 25 Japanese forces capture Hong Kong

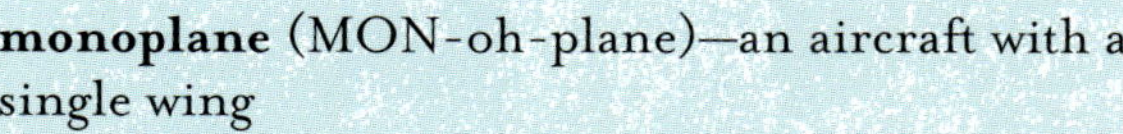

monoplane (MON-oh-plane)—an aircraft with a single wing

Nazi (NOT-see)—a member of Adolf Hitler's National Socialist Party

obliterate (uh-BLIT-uh-rate)—to destroy or wipe out utterly

offensive (uh-FEN-siv)—a planned military attack, often using large forces

paratrooper (PAIR-uh-troop-ur)—a soldier who deploys from an aircraft by parachute

pincer movement (PIN-sur MOOV-muhnt)—a military strategy designed to encircle and trap enemy forces

torpedo (tor-PEE-doh)—an underwater missile dropped from a plane or fired from a submarine in order to sink an enemy ship

uranium (yu-RAY-nee-uhm)—a type of rock that can be scientifically enriched to create the fuel for a nuclear weapon

war crime (WAR KRYM)—a crime against humanity, for example, deliberately killing unarmed prisoners or civilians during a war

Read More

Chandler, Matt. *Behind Enemy Lines: The Escape of Robert Grimes with the Comet Line.* Great Escapes of World War II. North Mankato, Minn.: Capstone Press, 2017.

Dickmann, Nancy. *The Horror of World War II.* Deadly History. North Mankato, Minn.: Capstone Press, 2018.

Doeden, Matt. *The Manhattan Project.* Heroes of World War II. Minneapolis: Lerner Publications, 2019.

Doeden, Matt. *Tuskegee Airmen.* Heroes of World War II. Minneapolis: Lerner Publications, 2019.

Owens, Lisa L. *Women Pilots of World War II.* Heroes of World War II. Minneapolis: Lerner Publications, 2019.

Internet Sites

The International Museum of World War II
https://museumofworldwarii.org

The National World War II Museum: New Orleans
https://www.nationalww2museum.org

Smithsonian National Air and Space Museum: World War II
https://airandspace.si.edu/topics/world-war-ii

1942

February 15 Japanese capture Singapore and take 60,000 Allied prisoners

April 2 Doolittle raid on Tokyo

May Battle of Bir Hakeim

June 4–7 U.S. Navy defeats Japanese at key Battle of Midway

July–November Australian forces battle with Japan on the Kokoda Trail in New Guinea

August Montgomery takes over Allied Eighth Army in North Africa

November 11 Allies defeat Afrika Korps at El Alamein

November Battle of Stalingrad begins

November 8 Operation Torch begins—U.S. troops land in North Africa; the Allies begin to close in on Axis forces

1943

February 2 Soviet forces defeat Nazi forces at Stalingrad

May 13 Axis forces surrender in North Africa; 275,000 taken prisoner

May 16 Dambusters raid on Ruhr, Germany

July 9 Allies invade Sicily

July–August Battle of Kursk

September 3 Allied forces invade Italy at Salerno

September 8 Italy surrenders; Nazi Germany now opposes Allied advance through Italy

1944

January 22 Allied forces land at Anzio, Italy

January–May Key battle of Monte Cassino in Italy

June 5 Rome liberated

June 6 D-Day—Allied armies invade Normandy to begin freeing Europe from Nazi forces

August 25 Paris liberated

October First Kamikaze attack

December 16 Battle of the Bulge begins—Nazi Germany launches its final, unsuccessful offensive in the Ardennes region of France

1945

March 23 Allied forces cross the Rhine River into Germany

April/May Soviet forces close in on Berlin; Hitler commits suicide on April 30 as the German capital falls

May 7 Nazi forces surrender

May 8 VE (Victory in Europe) Day—the war in Europe ends

August 6, August 9 United States drops atomic bombs on Hiroshima and Nagasaki, Japan

August 15 Japan surrenders; VJ (Victory over Japan) Day—the war in the Pacific ends

Index